THE DINÉ

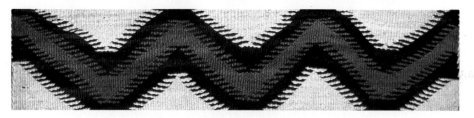

by Kathleen Cox

PEARSON

Scott
Foresman

Editorial Offices: Glenview, Illinois • Parsippany, New Jersey • New York, New York
Sales Offices: Needham, Massachusetts • Duluth, Georgia • Glenview, Illinois
Coppell, Texas • Ontario, California • Mesa, Arizona

Photographs

Every effort has been made to secure permission and provide appropriate credit for photographic material. The publisher deeply regrets any omission and pledges to correct errors called to its attention in subsequent editions.

Unless otherwise acknowledged, all photographs are the property of Pearson Education, Inc.

Photo locators denoted as follows: Top (T), Center (C), Bottom (B), Left (L), Right (R), Background (Bkgd)

ISBN: 0-328-13423-6

21 16

Long before Christopher Columbus, there were many groups of Native American people in North America. Some scholars think that thousands of years ago, their **ancestors** probably crossed from what is now Russia into what we now call Alaska. At that time a strip of land connected the two continents where the Bering Strait is today. The Diné, who are also known as the Navajo, were one of these groups of Native Americans.

The Diné may have **inhabited** the land that is now western Canada. They were hunters and gatherers. Diné ancestors did not have horses. They hunted on foot with spears and clubs. They also collected **edible** flowers, leaves, and roots of wild plants for food.

Native American ancestors probably crossed from Russia to Alaska where the Bering Strait is today.

The ancestors of the Diné were **nomads.** They never stayed in one area for very long. Since the Diné moved around, they had few possessions. They carried little more than their weapons and the simple tools they used for cooking. Too many possessions would slow them down.

Because they understood that their survival depended on the gifts of nature, the Diné might be called early **environmentalists.** They protected and respected the land. Never killing for sport, the Diné hunted only to get food for themselves. Very little of an animal was left behind. The Diné used animal skins for clothing, animal bones to create jewelry and weapons, and bird feathers for headgear.

The Diné's religion and folklore celebrated nature. They worshipped Father Sky and Mother Earth. They revered the mountains, the rainbow, the Sun, the rivers, and all animal species. Even plants were sacred to the Diné.

Over time the Diné drifted south through the Western plains. By the 1400s the Diné had migrated to the southwestern part of what is now the United States.

These carvings were found at the Canyon de Chelly in Arizona, where the Diné lived.

Part of the Southwest was a desert grassland. Though the area was very dry, part was covered with evergreen forests. Another part was thick with berry trees and nut trees. The Diné used the fibers of the beautiful yucca plant to weave sandals and baskets. Juniper and oak trees offered shade from the sun. The nuts from the pinion tree were good food.

Rock formations,
Monument Valley, Arizona

Beans

The Diné appreciated Mother Earth for all the wild animals—the many bears, mountain lions, mountain goats, elk, deer, rabbits, and raccoons. There were lots of birds, including eagles and wild turkeys, and plenty of fish in rivers.

In the Southwest the Diné discovered rivers and streams and the beauty of the land. Majestic rock formations stood like monuments inside huge canyons. Towering cliffs rose up on either side of narrow canyons. The beautiful land made the nature-loving nomads want to stay in one place.

The Southwest was also home to other Native Americans, including the Pueblo, who were farmers and lived in villages. When the Diné met the Pueblo, the Diné saw how these people benefited from planting corn, squash, and beans in nearby fields. These crops provided a steady source of food. The Pueblo taught the Diné how to make pottery. They showed them how to mix water into the clay dirt, mold the mixture, and fire it to make useful pots, containers, and tools.

The Diné learned the art of weaving from the Pueblo, who wove cloth from the cotton that they grew. The Diné used this cotton cloth to make more comfortable clothing for the hot summers. During the cold, snowy winters, the Diné continued to wear their warm animal skins.

In the 1600s Spanish explorers came to the Southwest. They traveled on powerful horses they had brought from Spain.

The Diné saw the strength and speed of these animals. They realized that it would be much easier to hunt on horses. They could travel much faster. Horses could also carry and pull heavy loads.

The Diné also admired the flocks of sheep that the Spanish had brought from Spain. The Diné realized that if they owned sheep, they would have a good supply of food. They would not have to hunt every day. The Diné decided they needed to get as many horses and sheep from the Spanish as they could.

The Diné raided the Spanish settlements. In time they became skilled raiders. They stole thousands of animals for their herds. The Diné liked how much these animals helped them in their everyday lives.

Raising livestock became important to the Diné.

The horse became the Diné's preferred way to travel, and sheep supplied much of their food. The Diné wove the wool from the sheep into warm blankets and rugs. In time the Diné became known as first-class weavers. They also were first-class raiders who raided other Native American settlements. Soon, many people feared the Diné.

A Diné woman weaves a rug.

The Spanish stirred up their own trouble with the Diné. The Spanish were devout Catholics. They wanted to turn the Diné into Catholics, but the Diné would not give up their sacred beliefs.

Fighting continued between the Diné and the Spanish. So, in time, the Diné moved to a remote part of the Southwest. They chose an area bordered by four mountains that cut into the sky from each of the four **cardinal points.** There was a towering peak in the north, in the east, in the south, and in the west. The Diné considered these four mountains sacred, along with the land within their boundaries.

This area was also a good hiding place for the Diné. Their scouts could conceal themselves behind rocks jutting up from the canyons, or they could hide out behind the rocky ledges on the top. When a warrior spotted trouble, there was plenty of time to signal other Diné to warn of danger.

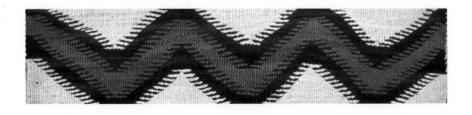

Peaks of La Plata Mountain (Dibé Nitsaa) in Colorado, one of
the four sacred mountains of Dinétah

The Diné called this rugged land Dinétah, or
homeland. For thousands of years small groups of
Diné had roamed North America. Usually, everyone
in each group was related. Once these small groups
moved to Dinétah, the Diné began to think of
themselves as a nation of people who shared a
common land.

Once the Diné got horses and sheep, their lifestyle changed. They continued to hunt, but now they hunted on horseback. They needed a constant source of food and water for the people and their herds.

The Diné farmed the surrounding land and grew crops of corn, squash, and beans. The Diné also grew splendid orchards of peach trees.

The Diné built **hogans.** Hogans were circular structures supported by logs or poles and normally covered with earth and bark. A fire was built inside for both heat and cooking. A smoke hole in the top of the hogan let smoke escape. The entrance to the hogan always faced east so the Diné could honor and greet the rising sun each morning. They lived in some of the hogans, but other hogans were used only for sacred ceremonies.

A Diné hogan

In the 1800s the population of the United States was expanding rapidly. People began settling in the Southwest. Soon, the Diné discovered they had a new rival: the U.S. cavalry and the American settlers.

The two groups battled each other off and on. Then, in 1846, the Diné signed a peace treaty with the U.S. government. Disagreements ended the peace by 1849.

A new general, James Henry Carleton, took control of the U.S. territory of New Mexico in 1862. The general decided he disliked Native Americans.

U.S. cavalry chasing Native Americans

Portrait of a Diné man

The general ordered Kit Carson, a famous trapper, hunter, and frontier scout, to defeat the Diné. The general told Carson that when the Diné surrendered to him, they would be taken from their homeland. Any Diné who didn't agree to surrender would be shot. The Diné soon discovered that they were fighting for their survival.

Carson rode his troops into Canyon de Chelly in Dinétah. Many Diné, who were starving, hid from them behind the rocks.

The Diné threw stones and spears at the invaders, but the cavalry had powerful rifles. The Diné could not stop their rivals from destroying the last of their peach trees and fields of corn, squash, and beans. They could not stop the destruction of their herds.

The Diné were overwhelmed and weak from many days with little food. They were exhausted from so many battles with the American soldiers. They were freezing from the harsh winter cold.

By the end of 1864, thousands of Diné had surrendered to the U.S. Army. Long lines of Diné men, women, and children walked about three hundred miles to Fort Sumner in New Mexico. The cavalry watched every step.

Many Diné died from starvation, illness, and exhaustion during the march, called the Long Walk. It took at least forty days for the Diné to get to Fort Sumner.

Once the Diné reached their new reservation, they continued to suffer. They tried to farm the new land, but the soil was poor. The weather was not much better. Part of the year brought no rain and too much sun, which dried out the land. The other part of the year brought floods from too much rain.

In four years, 25 percent of the Diné died from hunger and disease. The Diné who managed to survive those difficult years at Fort Sumner longed to return to their sacred homeland.

U.S. soldiers stand watch over the captured Diné at Fort Sumner.

Diné women weaving on their reservation

The U.S. government finally let the Diné sign a second peace treaty in 1868. In return the Diné were given land in the Southwest. Their new reservation included their sacred Dinétah. The Diné were also given some livestock to replace what had been taken. They were given the right to make their own laws on this new reservation. Their days of raiding were over. The Diné had to promise to keep the peace, and they could no longer fight against the U.S. government.

The cavalry had destroyed Dinétah. Weeds grew throughout the once-plowed fields, dirt filled the ditches where water once flowed, and the lovely peach trees were reduced to tree stumps. But the Diné still had their four sacred mountains.

The Diné wanted to repair the damage. They performed ceremonies in honor of their Mother Earth. They prayed that Mother Earth would bless them again. Over time the Diné made a comeback. By 1890 their population had doubled to eighteen thousand people. The Diné also increased the size of their reservation until they owned more than fifteen million acres of land. Most of their land is in New Mexico and Arizona. The Diné also built up their livestock.

In the 1940s the Diné joined forces with the people who once captured them. More than three thousand Diné became members of the U.S. military during World War II. Many of them trained to become Code Talkers. The Code Talkers were Marines stationed in the Pacific.

World War II Code Talkers

The Code Talkers did not fight with guns. They fought with their language. The Diné sent important secret messages to other Marines so that they could defeat the Japanese. The Japanese, who had skilled code-breakers, could not understand the secret Diné code.

Since World War II, the Diné nation has worked to create new opportunities for its people and the country. The Diné are allowing oil wells on their land, and already companies are searching for valuable minerals.

The Diné teach their children to respect their culture, and they want them to know the Diné nation's history. They want them to learn their language and to revere their land and traditions—to have a respect for the old teachings. People across America also have learned to respect and understand the Diné culture, as it is a special part of our diverse country.

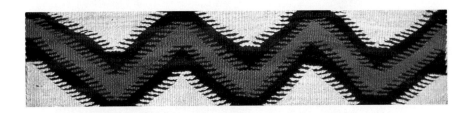

Now Try This

Be a First-Class Weaver

The Diné are known for their beautiful weaving work. As you know, they wove cotton into cool clothing and wool into warm blankets and rugs. The skilled art of weaving is an important part of the Diné culture. Their artistry represents who they are as a people. You can be a first-class weaver too!

Diné woven blanket

Here's How to Do It!

1. Find two same-sized pieces of construction paper in two of your favorite colors.

2. Cut one piece of paper into one-inch-wide strips going the long way, shown in example A. Cut the other piece of paper into one-inch-wide strips going the short way, shown in example B, leaving the last inch of the strip connected to the paper. This will be your base to start weaving.

3. Weave the strips of the first piece of paper over and under the strips of the second piece of paper. If one row begins by going "over," then the next row should begin by going "under." This will create your pattern. You may want to use small pieces of tape on the last strip to keep it in place.

4. Try experimenting with thinner or wider strips. Try different colors to make unique designs. Decorate your woven art with symbols that represent who you are as a person.

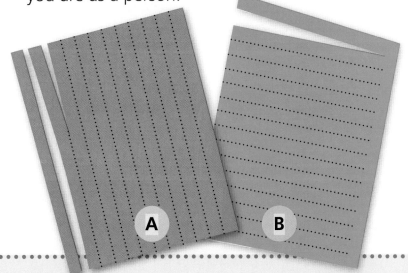

A

B

Glossary

ancestors *n.* people from whom you are descended, such as your great-grandparents.

cardinal points *n.* an expression for the four principal directions on the compass: north, south, east, and west.

edible *adj.* something that is safe to eat.

environmentalists *n.* people who want to protect the land.

hogans *n.* circular buildings, made from logs and earth, used by the Diné.

inhabited *v.* lived in a place.

nomads *n.* people who move from place to place.